PROFILES

Alexander Fleming

Josephine Ross

Illustrated by
Edward Mortelmans

Hamish Hamilton
London

First published 1984 by
Hamish Hamilton Children's Books
Garden House, 57-59 Long Acre, London WC2E 9JZ
© 1984 text by Josephine Ross
© 1984 illustrations by Edward Mortelmans
All rights reserved
British Library Cataloguing in Publication Data
Ross, Josephine
Alexander Fleming. — (Profiles)
1. Fleming, *Sir* Alexander — Juvenile literature
2. Bacteriologists — Great Britain —
Biography — Juvenile literature   3. Penicillin
— History — Juvenile literature
I. Title   II. Series
616'.014'0924   QR31.F5
ISBN 0-241-11203-6
Typeset by Pioneer
Printed in Great Britain at the
University Press, Cambridge

For my godson, Edward Ridge

Contents

Saying goodbye to Lochfield

1   A Scottish Boyhood

Towards the end of the last century, a fourteen-year-old boy left his home near the town of Darvel, in Scotland, and began the long journey south, to London. Alec Fleming was small for his age, but sturdy and quick-witted, and he had done well at the local schools; his widowed mother believed that the great, crowded, Victorian city held brighter prospects for a clever boy than the isolated lowlands around Darvel.

Yet as Mrs Grace Fleming said goodbye to her son on that summer day in 1895, even she could scarcely have dreamed of the career which lay ahead of him. One day, not only London but cities throughout the world, from Bombay to Rio de Janeiro, would welcome Sir Alexander Fleming with waving flags, cheering crowds and red-carpet receptions. His name would appear on street-signs and statues; international honours, from a Nobel Prize for medicine to the honorary chiefship of an Indian tribe would be heaped upon him — even a Fleming Crater on the Moon called after him. As the discoverer of the lifesaving 'miracle' drug, penicillin, the boy from Darvel was destined to become one of the most famous men in the world.

By a strange coincidence, Alexander Fleming's birth, on 6 August 1881, took place in the same year as another major medical breakthrough. It was in 1881, in France, that the great scientist Louis Pasteur showed the world the importance of vaccination as a means of preventing diseases. Yet despite such advances, medicine when Fleming was a boy bore little resemblance to the medical science of today. Without modern drugs, such as penicillin and other antibiotics, even such everyday illnesses as tonsillitis could be fatal. Scarlet fever — easily controlled today with penicillin — killed thousands of children every year. Such unchecked disease, combined with poor diet and lack of hygiene, helped to reduce the average lifespan of a British man or woman, at the time of Fleming's birth, to under fifty years — compared with seventy-odd years in the 1980s.

The Fleming children were fortunate: unlike those living in the huddled slums of Victorian cities, they grew up in the clear air of Ayrshire, where life was hard but healthy. They were a large family. Their father, Hugh Fleming, was already an elderly widower with four children when he married his second wife, Grace, in 1876. With her he had four more — a daughter, also named Grace, followed by John, Alexander (always known as Alec), and Robert. Mrs Grace Fleming, a wise and loving woman, treated all eight children as her own; and though money was scarce and she had her hands full cooking, washing and bringing up so many youngsters, she made a happy home for them all. 'She was always ready to join in any fun we were having,' Robert later recalled.

Lochfield Farm, Alexander Fleming's birthplace, was a low stone farmhouse set on a lonely hillside a few kilometres outside Darvel. It belonged to the Earl of Loudoun, a local landowner, but Hugh Fleming lived and farmed there as his tenant, raising sheep, crops and some cattle on the bleak 300-odd hectares. Like most country children, Alec spent much of his time out

Guddling for trout

of doors. When he and his brothers and sisters were not helping with the haymaking, or watching the lambing on the farm, they would ramble for hours among the heather-covered hills and moorland around their home. They liked to fish for trout — sometimes even 'guddling', or tickling them — and often returned with a rabbit which they had caught, to add to the family food supplies.

Winter brought harsh winds and thick snow to Lochfield. In the evenings, clustered together by the light of paraffin lamps, the children invented stories and played Victorian parlour games, or made up new ones. They were not a bookish family; in adult life, Alexander Fleming preferred a good thriller to any other reading. But they were imaginative. 'We had to make our own amusements, but that was easy in such surroundings,' Fleming later wrote. One of their games nearly ended in disaster for Alec: rolling down a steep hill, for fun, he suddenly found that he was tumbling towards a sheer precipice at the bottom. Somehow he stopped in time, and bounced up, saying cheerfully, 'I cam' down that quick!' in his broad Scots accent.

When the warm weather came, the young Flemings often took off their boots and stockings and walked the kilometre or so to school barefoot. Loudoun Moor School, where Alec went at the age of five, consisted of one classroom and less than a dozen pupils, but it gave them a good grounding in such basic subjects as reading and arithmetic. Alec Fleming enjoyed his early schooling, and without seeming to take any trouble over his lessons, he learned fast. 'A dear little boy with dreamy blue eyes' was how one of his teachers later described him.

Despite the dreamy eyes, Alec Fleming was a tough youngster. In 1891, when he was ten, he was sent to a larger school, in Darvel; to get there he had to walk six kilometres each morning, with another six-kilometre walk home. On cold days his mother gave him two hot baked potatoes to carry, to keep his hands warm. But

Alec's nose is broken

twelve kilometres a day, in all weathers, was a long trudge for a schoolboy. However, he made the best of it, and said later that the daily journey had given him ideal opportunities for nature study, as well as building up his health and stamina — all useful assets in a medical career. There was another, less pleasant, legacy from his Darvel schooldays: in a playground accident, colliding with another boy, Alec's nose was broken. He had a battered profile for the rest of his life.

At twelve, Alec changed school again, and became one of 700 or so pupils at the Kilmarnock Academy. Kilmarnock was too far even for Alec to walk, so he boarded with a relation who lived in the big industrial town, and returned home to Lochfield only once a week. Like most Victorian families, the Flemings believed in making sacrifices for the sake of education, and the Academy was a fine school. Tom Fleming, the second of Alec's older half-brothers, had gone on from there to study medicine at Glasgow University.

But if Alec had any boyhood hopes of following Tom's example, and one day becoming a doctor, it seemed they were doomed to disappointment. Circumstances at Lochfield had changed during Alec's childhood. The death of Hugh Fleming in 1888, when Alec was seven, had caused the tenancy of the farm to pass to his oldest half-brother, who was also named Hugh. It was he who, with Alec's mother Grace, now provided for the younger Flemings, and helped to plan their futures. Only eighteen months after Alec entered Kilmarnock Academy, it was decided that he should leave. A greater change was in store for him.

Tom Fleming, the doctor half-brother, had gone down to London, where he had set up in practice as an oculist — treating problems of the eye. Alec's elder brother John had joined him, to lodge in his rented house at No. 144 Marylebone Road, and learn a trade with a firm of spectacle-makers — a job which Tom had found for him. In 1895 it was decided that young Alec should also go south, to complete his studies in London, and try to find employment.

And so it was that, at the age of fourteen, Alexander Fleming set out on the first stage of his remarkable career. He would return to Lochfield Farm for visits, and in later years he told the people of Darvel, 'My heart is still with you, and with the moors beyond.' But for the rest of his life, London was to be his home.

Arriving in London

2   London Life

To the Scottish farm boy newly arrived in the big city,
London, with its 4½ million inhabitants, must have
seemed a different world. Instead of wide, tranquil
hills dotted with sheep, Alec now found himself
surrounded by crowded pavements and noisy streets
filled with horse-drawn traffic. Steam-driven under-
ground trains rattled beneath his feet; the sky he
glimpsed through the rooftops was grey with chimney-
smoke; and the quick patter of Cockney voices replaced
the soft, familiar Scots accents of his faraway home. Yet
it was all new and exciting for an adventurous boy, and
Alec settled in quickly.

Six months after his arrival, his younger brother
Robert also joined the London household, and together
the boys went exploring. Instead of 'guddling' for trout,
or chasing rabbits across the heather, they now rode on
open-topped buses, visited museums and the theatre,
and saw the sights, such as Westminster Abbey, the
newly-built Tower Bridge (a marvel of Victorian
engineering) and Regent's Park Zoo. In St Paul's
Cathedral they gazed on the memorials to Britain's
heroes — little knowing that Alec himself would one
day have a place there, beside Nelson and Wellington.

Though Tom Fleming's medical practice began to
prosper, and John enjoyed making spectacles, there
was still no suggestion of a medical career for Alec.
Instead, he seemed destined for a future in a city office.
At the Regent Street Polytechnic, the London college
to which both he and Robert were sent, they went into

the commercial classes, learning such skills as book-keeping along with the ordinary school subjects. As usual, Alec appeared to do well without any effort. His early schooling in Scotland had put him ahead of his new classmates, and even exams came easily to him.

In 1897, at the age of sixteen, Alec Fleming left the Polytechnic and went into his first job — in a city shipping office. He was now almost grown-up. With his short, strong build (he never grew above 1.65m) and broken nose, he looked rather like a boxer; but his mop of thick, light hair and remarkably large blue eyes made him an attractive young man. Alec always had a quiet manner, seeming to weigh up people and situations before he spoke — yet to those he knew well he was a loyal friend, and beneath his reserved air there lurked a keen sense of fun.

At work, he had little chance to enjoy himself. As a junior clerk with the famous America Line, a company which ran ocean liners across the North Atlantic, he was paid 10 shillings a week — which, he glumly worked out, was about tuppence-halfpenny per hour (1p today). To earn it, he spent his days in an office in Leadenhall Street, keeping records of passengers and cargoes, writing out accounts and copying documents by hand. For a boy of his abilities it was dull work, and he must have been glad to get home in the evenings.

The Fleming household was a cheerful place. From 144 Marylebone Road, Dr Tom Fleming moved to larger premises at 29 York Street, next to Baker Street. Here, after work, the family kept up their old tradition of playing endless games — trying everything from

17

Working in the shipping office

ping-pong to poker. Sometimes Tom organised quizzes and competitions; he once even tried to teach his brothers boxing. But they had only one pair of boxing gloves between them and Mary, Tom's younger sister who kept house for them all, decided that the bouts were spoiling the happy atmosphere, so that particular sport had to be abandoned.

It was in the year 1900 that an important new interest came into Alec's life — and took him, by another strange quirk of fate, a step closer to his eventual career. It all began with the 'Boer War', between the Dutch and British settlers in South Africa. When, early in 1900, the Dutch 'Boers' seemed likely to take over the British Empire's South African possessions, a wave of patriotic fervour swept the British Isles.

The garrison of Mafeking was under siege and volunteers were needed for the army. In London, two of the young men who eagerly offered themselves as part-time soldiers were John and Alec Fleming. As recruits to the London Scottish Rifle Volunteers, they spent all their available hours in marching, drilling and training. It was a life which Alec found very much to his liking.

Even when the crisis ended, without any of the Flemings being sent abroad, Alec remained an enthusiastic territorial soldier. In the London Scottish he could mix with fellow-Scotsmen far from home; and as well as a good social life, the regiment offered excellent opportunities for sport. Alec discovered unexpected talents in himself. Both he and Robert — who joined the London Scottish in 1901, at eighteen — became good rifle shots, taking part in national competitions. They also took up water-polo. And it was a game of water-polo which Alec played for the regiment, against a team from St Mary's Hospital, Paddington, which decided the course of his future.

Under the will of a bachelor uncle, who had recently died, each of the young Flemings inherited £250 — a considerable sum of money. To Alec, especially, it represented the chance of a whole new life. His eldest half-brother, Hugh, was happy farming at Lochfield; Tom was doing well as an oculist; John enjoyed the optical business, and so did Robert, who had joined him. But Alec's job in the city had never suited his talents. Here was his opportunity. He would give it up — and use his legacy to become a doctor.

Whether his decision was the result of a real interest in medicine, or whether, at this stage, he was influenced by Tom's example, once Alec's mind was made up he would not be put off. He lacked the necessary diploma which would qualify him for medical school, and he had not learned Latin; so he promptly found himself a tutor in Latin, and with Tom's help, arranged to sit for the diploma. He took his exams in July 1901 — and came out equal top of all the candidates.

All that remained was to choose which London medical school he should join. Then, as now, there were twelve of them, attached to London University, and all were famous institutions. According to Fleming's own account, he had no special preference — but he had once played water-polo against St Mary's Hospital, Paddington. And so, in the autumn of 1901, it was to St Mary's that the young Alexander Fleming went.

Learning to shoot with the London Scottish Rifle Volunteers

3 The Medical Student

St Mary's, Paddington, where Fleming was to train, work and make his great discovery, was the newest of the London teaching hospitals. Founded in 1845 (the oldest, St Bartholomew's, dates from the 12th century), it stood in Praed Street, beside Paddington Station. Paddington was then one of London's poorer districts. Noise and grime from the railway added to the bad living conditions, and disease of all kinds flourished among the local population — providing grim practical experience for the student doctors at St Mary's.

Whatever Alec's reasons had been for taking up medicine, and choosing St Mary's, it soon became obvious that he had made the right decision. Though, at twenty, he was two years older than most of his fellow-students, and came from a very different background, he fitted in easily with college life, joining societies, taking part in his favourite sports of rifle-shooting and water-polo, and acting in amateur dramatics. And he quickly showed himself to be a brilliant student. Alec had always found learning easy; now that the work interested him, he shone.

According to Robert Fleming, who wrote a memoir of his brother's early life, Alec could read a text-book at a glance, skipping over the pages and groaning loudly if he spotted a mistake by the author. But although Fleming was rarely seen to work hard, he regularly came top of his class. In his first year at St Mary's, he not only won prizes for chemistry and biology, he was also awarded a scholarship which paid his first-year

At medical school

fees. They were the first of many successes for the future Nobel Prize-winner.

In Alec's student days (and for most of his career) there was no National Health Service to run the nation's hospitals and provide free health care for all. Just as doctors had to pay for their training, the sick paid for their own treatment. Those who were too poor could be admitted to the public wards of a voluntary hospital where their costs were met by charitable funds. St Mary's was constantly short of money, and though the standard of teaching was high, conditions in the Medical School were spartan.

Sitting on hard benches in chilly lecture-rooms, the students spent their first three years learning the theory of medicine. They could not yet treat actual patients, but they learned anatomy (the structure of the human body) by cutting up dead bodies. Anatomy interested Fleming. He won the Senior Anatomy Prize, and thought of becoming a surgeon once he had qualified.

Having passed the Intermediate MB exam with flying colours, in 1904, Alec began his 'clinical' training, dealing with patients. In the Outpatients department he gave on-the-spot treatment, such as stitching wounds, taking out teeth and setting broken bones. And in the hospital wards, under the guidance of senior doctors, he examined the sick, learning to diagnose symptoms and recommend treatment.

Many of the worst cases in the wards were suffering from illnesses rarely seen today — those caused by bacterial infections. The connection of bacteria, minute organisms found throughout Nature, with disease had at last been proved, notably through the work of Louis Pasteur; and the need for inoculation, to protect human beings against harmful types of bacteria, had begun to be accepted. But inoculation was not yet widely available, and for those who had been struck down by one of the serious bacterial infections, there was little any doctor could do. Diseases which can be cured by modern drugs, such as pneumonia and tuberculosis, were common killers in the early 1900s. Even a simple cut finger could be highly dangerous, if bacteria got into the wound.

By one of the strange twists of fate in Fleming's career, soon after he entered St Mary's as a student, a leading expert in bacteriology (the study of bacteria) had joined the staff. Almroth Wright, the new Professor of Pathology, was an impressive figure. Tall, shaggy-haired and bear-like in appearance, he was famed for his forceful opinions and eccentric ways. But he had a brilliant mind, and he had dedicated his life and career to the struggle against disease. Alec, the quiet cautious Scot, and the strong-willed Professor did not always see eye-to-eye: Alec once described a lecture by Wright as 'a lot of hot air'. But he could not fail to be inspired by Wright's ideas and teaching.

As a student, it seems Alec had no plans to become a bacteriologist himself. He was attracted to surgery, and in 1905 he took the first part of the Royal College of Surgeons' exams. His medical training was almost completed. Having gained his experience in obstetrics, delivering babies in the poor, overcrowded dwellings of Paddington's back streets, he took his medical finals in the summer of 1906, and passed, in his usual effortless style. At the age of twenty-five, Alexander Fleming was a qualified doctor.

A number of choices were now open to him. He could go straight into practice as a GP, a local, general doctor; he could find himself an appointment at one of the other hospitals; or he could stay on at St Mary's and study for a further qualification, the MB BS exams, which would leave him more highly-equipped to choose his future career. Once again, fate stepped in.

One of Sir Almroth Wright's research team, a doctor named John Freeman, was a keen rifle-shot. He was anxious to keep Alec Fleming at St Mary's for the sake of the hospital rifle-team, and so he came up with an

Almroth Wright, Professor of Pathology at St Mary's Hospital, Paddington

idea. Wright needed a new assistant in the Bacteriology department — why should not Alec take up the post, part-time, whilst working for his higher exams? The small salary would pay his student expenses, and the experience would be useful.

A game of water-polo had brought Fleming to St Mary's; now a talent for rifle-shooting decided his future. In the summer of 1906 he joined Wright's department, as a temporary measure. He was to stay there for almost fifty years.

4 The Inoculation Department

'Of all the evils that befall Man', Sir Almroth Wright once wrote in a newspaper article, 'the evil of disease is incomparably the greatest.' In his department at St Mary's Hospital, surrounded by a group of dedicated research workers, he tirelessly carried on the battle against the 'greatest evil'.

When Alexander Fleming joined Wright's team — as he thought, on a temporary basis — it was housed in two shabby and inadequate rooms. But as Wright's fame spread, so did the department; and in 1908 it moved to more spacious laboratories, overlooking Praed Street. Here, with the help of private donations, income from the sale of vaccines and fees from patients who came to be treated by Wright, 'The Inoculation Department', as it was called, began to flourish.

At first Alec Fleming did not play a major role in the life of the Department. He had his exams to think of; and in his usual way he worked hard and said little. But 'Little Flem', as he was nicknamed, soon became generally liked. Wright — himself a brilliant talker — often teased Fleming about his habit of remaining silent when spoken to, and tried to draw him out on such topics as poetry and the Bible. Alec's dry sense of humour was more than equal to these combats, however, and his obvious skills earned even Wright's respect.

Some of the laboratory equipment then in daily use had to be made by the researchers themselves. Alec had always been good with his hands; he now showed a

In the lab

talent for making such implements as the delicate 'pipettes', or fine-stemmed glass tubes which could be used to suck up fluids for an experiment, or deposit them drop by drop on microscope slides. Sometimes, to please a child or a visitor, Alec would fashion glass animals, such as cats and mice.

Among the other tools of the trade on Alec's cluttered laboratory bench were 'Petri dishes' (glass containers with lids, in which bacteria were cultivated on gelatine). A swab, or sample, of human fluid (such as blood, or spit) could be put in a Petri dish and left to develop, with the lid closed to prevent any other germs getting in. From the various bacteria which would appear, the one required could then be identified, removed, and made into a vaccine.

At home, Alec was always taking swabs from his family if one of them had a cough or cold, and testing vaccines on himself and his brothers. Fortunately, as Robert recorded, Alec was good at giving injections painlessly. And, perhaps as a result of their healthy, open-air upbringing, none of them seemed to suffer from being used as guinea-pigs.

Since Alec first joined St Mary's, there had been changes in the Fleming family. Up in Scotland, to the delight of them all, Hugh Fleming had married; and so Mrs Grace Fleming had left Lochfield Farm and come south, to look after the London branch of the family. At first, she and the younger sons went to live in Ealing. But then Mrs Fleming found a large flat at number 125 Clarence Gate Gardens, near Regent's Park, and John, Alec and Robert moved with her. For John and Robert, who were now running their own successful optical business, and Alec, who needed to be near St Mary's, the Clarence Gate Gardens flat was convenient; and Tom was a regular visitor there, so the family was as close as ever.

In the spring of 1908 Alec sat for his final MB BS exams, and not only passed, but was awarded the London University Gold medal for his performance. He still wanted to qualify in surgery, however, so in the following year he took the second part of the Royal

Learning to appreciate art

College of Surgeons exam — and passed. Yet, having equipped himself to practise surgery, he never took it up. It seemed by 1909 that Fleming had come to a decision: he would stay with the happy, close-knit team in the Inoculation Department and devote himself to the vital work of bacteriology.

Already Alec had begun to publish articles in medical journals, such as *The Lancet*, and it was not long before the young Scots doctor began to make a name for himself. He developed a new form of blood-test for one infection; and his success in applying treatments and preparing vaccines brought him an increasing number of private patients, who added to his modest salary from the Department.

Socially, as well as professionally, young Dr Fleming now found himself in demand. Despite his reserved manner, which could be off-putting to strangers, he loved good company and parties — and, of course, all kinds of games. He made friends with an artistic family, called the Pegrams, and through them he met a circle which included painters, illustrators and novelists. One of them, the well-known painter Ronald Gray, became a particular friend, after Alec successfully treated him for tuberculosis of the knee. The grateful Mr Gray introduced Alec to a famous and exclusive society called The Chelsea Arts Club, whose members met one another to enjoy fine dinners, conversation and relaxations such as billiards and croquet. Officially, only artists could join — but Alec was appointed their 'Honorary Bacteriologist', and became one of their most popular members. He went several times to the club's annual fancy dress party, the Chelsea Arts Ball; one year he appeared dressed as a little girl, to his own and his friends' amusement.

In fact, Fleming did have a talent for painting. And he found a way of growing bacteria in different colours, so that they formed a picture. Some of his designs, of ballet-dancers, or soldiers, were exquisite − and all done with bacteria. Sir Almroth Wright remarked half-seriously that Alec even treated research 'like a game', which had a grain of truth in it. Fleming enjoyed his work, and he brought to the serious study of bacteria an original mind and an imaginative approach, without which he might never have made the great discovery of penicillin.

Working in the Department, seeing his own patients, and keeping up a full social life, Alec had little time left for his other interest − the London Scottish Regiment. In the spring of 1914 he finally decided that he would have to give it up altogether; and so, after thirteen happy years, he regretfully resigned.

But his army days were far from over. Before the end of that year, all Europe was at war − and Alec Fleming was in uniform again.

5   In War and Peace

The First World War began in August 1914, when Great Britain finally declared war on the power-hungry Kaiser of Germany. Among those who hastened to offer their services in the coming struggle was Sir Almroth Wright.

Wright had experience of army medicine. During the Boer War he had waged a desperate campaign to have the soldiers inoculated against the killer disease of typhoid fever, with little success. Now he urged the necessity of vaccinating the men who were to fight in the Great War — and this time he won. Among the terrible toll of casualties in the 1914-18 War, at least there were to be few deaths from typhoid in the British forces.

Millions of other cases of injury and illness would require urgent treatment, however, and medical skills of all kinds were needed in the army. It was decided that Wright should set up a special department, near to the fighting in France, to study the problems of infected wounds and try to remedy them. And so, in the autumn of 1914, Wright and his team of bacteriologists were sent over to Boulogne, to establish their unit in part of a military hospital. Wright was made a Lieutenant-Colonel; Alec Fleming, who had never risen above the rank of Private in the London Scottish, accompanied him, as a Lieutenant.

They were based in a former casino, where before the War the rich had gone to gamble; but there was nothing pleasurable about the surroundings now. In

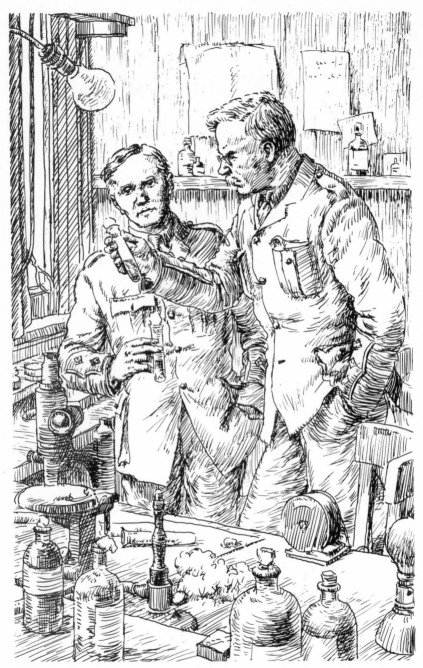

Fleming and Wright in France during the First World War

what had been a fencing room on the top floor, the bacteriologists had to create a working laboratory with the minimum of equipment; whilst in the wards below a never-ending stream of the injured and dying lay waiting for treatment. As yet there was no drug which would cure bacterial infection, once it attacked a wound. Many of those brought in from the battlefields died, not of their actual wounds, but from the infections which set in afterwards.

At Boulogne, Alec worked relentlessly, taking swabs from the wounded, identifying the groups of bacteria, and studying their behaviour. Army surgeons at that time clung to the belief that powerful antiseptics would hold the key to healing infections in wounds. But Fleming and Wright proceeded to show otherwise. The wrong antiseptics, Alec demonstrated, in a paper published in 1915, would actually suppress the patient's own internal defences, while allowing the bacteria to thrive. The best treatment lay in cleansing with a simple solution which would stimulate the body's natural healing process. All the same, many of the injured could not be saved, and it was a deeply distressing period in Fleming's career.

To his private life, however, the war-years brought a sudden, and unexpected, source of happiness. Just before Christmas 1915, whilst on leave in England, Alec got married. In some ways, his choice of a bride was surprising. Sally McElroy, the new Mrs Fleming, was a bright, lively Irish girl, who presented a striking contrast to her short, silent husband. But they had a great deal in common, including medicine: Sally was a trained nurse, who ran her own nursing-home, and Alec loved her strong, competent personality. To add to their happiness, Alec's elder brother John and Sally's twin sister Elizabeth proceeded to fall in love, and marry. As ever, close family links were important to the Flemings.

When the War ended, on 11 November 1918, its horrors were not yet over. A massive, international epidemic of 'flu had begun to sweep across the world, killing some 20 million people in all. The hospital at Boulogne was crowded with cases, presenting fresh work for the bacteriologists. Not until early 1919 could Alec return to London, to his old life at St Mary's — and his new life with Sally.

It was while they were staying with friends in Suffolk, in 1921, that Alec and Sally chanced upon the house which was to be the setting for some of their happiest times. Called The Dhoon, it was a pretty 18th-century house, not too big, with a large garden and even a stream in which Alec could fish, as once he had 'guddled' for trout. Here the Flemings spent their weekends, working in the garden — where anything seemed to grow for Alec — entertaining family and friends, and swimming in the river. As always there were games, particularly croquet, which they played until late at night, by candle-light — usually with hilarious new rules invented by Alec. As his brother Robert — a frequent visitor to The Dhoon — once observed, there was always 'something of the boy' in Alexander Fleming.

In London, they acquired a flat in Danvers Street,

The surgical wards at Boulogne

which was convenient for Alec's beloved Chelsea Arts Club. But after the birth of their son in 1924, whom they christened Robert, Sally liked to spend as much time as possible at The Dhoon. Little Robert was usually surrounded by his Fleming cousins, the children of Alec's brothers, and in Suffolk he enjoyed something of the carefree outdoor life his father had known as a boy. Mrs Fleming preferred not to be known as 'Aunt Sally' by the children; she took on the Irish nickname of 'Sareen' instead, and remained Sareen for the rest of her life.

In his private life, Alec had found happiness; and at work he was on the brink of a great discovery.

6 The Great Discovery

A newcomer who joined the Inoculation Department
in 1921 was often teased by Alec Fleming for being
much too tidy. The younger man, Dr Allison, liked to
clear his laboratory bench at the end of the day, and
throw away the cultures from completed experiments.
Fleming's approach was quite different. He would leave
his experimental cultures long after they were finished

Fleming's workbench

with, until his bench was crowded with old test tubes and Petri dishes. Only then would he have his equipment washed out and sterilised, ready for re-use — having first checked each plate, to make quite sure it contained nothing of interest. If Fleming had been 'tidy', like young Dr Allison, he might never have found penicillin.

Fleming's first great breakthrough came with a different discovery, in the early 1920s. He had had a cold, and out of interest had cultivated a swab of catarrh from his nose to see what would develop. Accidentally, bacteria had drifted onto the dish containing the catarrh-culture; and after a time, as Fleming showed Dr Allison, a startling result could be seen. Around the nasal fluid, the invading bacteria simply vanished. Something in the human catarrh had overcome them.

Greatly excited, Alec tried a number of experiments. He took samples from friends' noses, and discovered that the bacteria-killing reaction was always present, and was not the result of a cold. Then he went on to other body fluids, such as tears and pus — and found the same effect: something in them dissolved certain outside bacteria. It became a standing joke that everyone who went into the Department had to contribute some tears for the tests. Lemon juice was kept handy to prick visitors' eyes into watering, and a cartoon appeared in *Punch* magazine showing schoolboys being beaten, to make them cry for Fleming's experiments. What Fleming had found was a natural, anti-bacterial substance, protecting the body by a process of 'lysis' (the dissolving of cells or bacteria). Sir Almroth

'Another method of obtaining Lysozyme, the antiseptic contained in tears'.

From a cartoon by J. H. Dowd (courtesy of *Punch*, 1922).

Wright, who was a Greek scholar, loved playing with words, and he gave the newly-identified substance its name: lysozyme.

Unfortunately for Alec, his finding did not, at the time, receive the attention it deserved. This was partly because it did not seem to work against the bacteria which caused mankind's most serious diseases; and partly because Fleming was bad at communicating his ideas in public. His lectures on lysozyme were badly delivered, in a flat voice without any trace of his personality or humour; and even experienced medical men found them hard to grasp. However, with the assistance of Dr Allison, Fleming continued his work on lysozyme for several years — and even when relaxing at The Dhoon he busily gathered samples of garden plants and different species of fish from the river, to investigate their lysozyme content. Today, the importance of lysozyme is recognised; it is already used in connection with the preserving of some foods, and the research still goes on.

Though the 1920s marked the most important years of Fleming's career, he still had plenty of time to enjoy his family and social life. Weekends were spent at The Dhoon, and on weekday evenings he usually visited his club before going home to Chelsea. Even in the laboratory he liked to have company about him — though, as always, he said little himself, preferring to listen to others.

The door to his small, cluttered laboratory at St Mary's was always kept open, so visitors could drop in; and it was one such caller who had the good fortune to

The small lab at The Dhoon

be present at the moment of Alexander Fleming's great discovery, in the autumn of 1928.

A former researcher from the department, named Pryce, dropped in one September day to see how some work he had been involved in was progressing. There on Fleming's crowded bench lay the usual piles of Petri dishes containing past experiments, about to be sterilised, washed and re-used. From these Fleming picked out one or two to show to Pryce, glancing at them first. Suddenly he looked surprised. 'That's funny!' he said, and peered more closely. On the plate he was holding, a patch of mould had appeared — and around the blob of mould, an extraordinary reaction could be seen. The plate contained a particularly harmful type of bacteria, which normally lay in small yellow colonies. But where the germs were in contact with the mould, they had apparently melted away, leaving a clear area. A simple blob of mould was killing the bacteria.

What Fleming and Pryce were witnessing, in that moment, was the effect of penicillin. From this discovery of the powers of a certain species of everyday mould would come one of the most valuable drugs in mankind's struggle against disease. Yet at the time, scarcely anyone realised its significance.

Pryce agreed that the effect was very strange, and went on his way. Other members of the Department to whom Fleming showed his mouldy culture dish over the next few days were unimpressed. 'They thought it was just one of my toys', Fleming recalled, years later. He always referred to the discovery as simply 'a chance

44

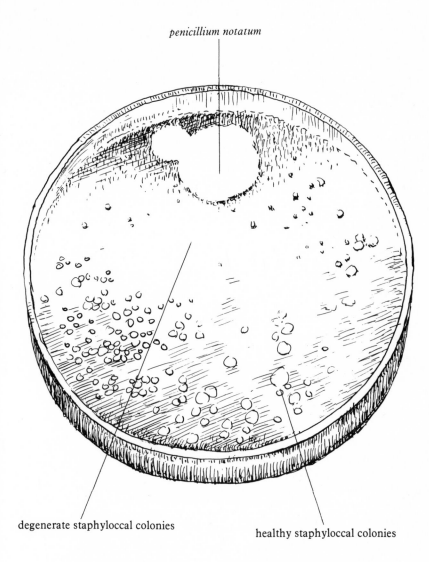

penicillium notatum

degenerate staphyloccal colonies

healthy staphyloccal colonies

Petri dish showing original mould growth of *Penicillium notatum*

observation'; and indeed the strokes of luck, and sheer coincidences, involved in the finding of penicillin were almost miraculous. Somehow, a few spores of the right species of mould had drifted into the laboratory, to land in a culture dish sown with one of the disease-causing types of bacteria against which it would be effective. And then, instead of washing out the discarded dish, Fleming happened to pick it up again, and look at it closely. Against all the odds, he had found 'the antiseptic of his dreams' — penicillin. It was an historic moment.

7   The Miracle Drug

From Fleming's first observation of a mouldy Petri dish in his laboratory at St Mary's, to the production of penicillin as a drug available to all, was a long haul. It took time, faith and many people's skills to turn the 'chance observation' into a real, effective cure for human disease.

The initial lack of interest shown by his colleagues did nothing to dampen Fleming's excitement over his discovery. In the months that followed, he set out to investigate its possibilities. Since the mould was of the *Penicillium notatum* variety, its extract was given the name of 'penicillin'; and research into penicillin now took up much of Alec's time.

Other moulds were tested, to see if they had similar effects, and for weeks Alec went around collecting samples from mouldy food, old boots and clothing, and stray dust. But none of them showed anti-bacterial powers like those of the original penicillium. The penicillin itself was tested for side-effects — and shown to be safe for the surfaces of human eyes and wounds, despite its effect on bacteria. And the range of germs against which it appeared to work included many of the bacteria most dangerous to mankind. The problems lay in finding a way to harness the powers of this remarkable substance, and turn it into a drug which could be produced in large quantities.

Fleming was a bacteriologist, not a chemist; and though he had brought penicillin to the attention of the world, it would be left to others, with different

Florey and Chain

practical skills, to develop his finding. Having eagerly researched into penicillin, and published an important paper on the subject towards the end of 1929, he began to turn his attention towards other work. Despite the strong signs that penicillin had anti-bacterial powers, early trials on patients were inconclusive; and the problem of keeping the substance active for long enough to allow it to destroy germs in the body seemed, at this time, unsolvable.

It was not until 1939, eleven years after Fleming made his discovery, that the research into penicillin as a cure began again in earnest — at Oxford. There, in the University's pathology department, the Australian-born Professor Howard Florey took on the challenge of investigating penicillin, assisted by a brilliant European refugee named Ernst Chain. 'Florey was always a great finisher', it was said; now, backed by a meagre initial grant of £25, Florey and Chain set out to finish the work begun by Fleming.

The outbreak of the Second World War, in August 1939, brought grim reminders of the previous war and the hazards of wound infection. But in the spring of 1940, as Nazi Germany stood poised to invade Britain, Florey and Chain made the breakthrough: they proved that penicillin could protect animals from deadly infections. They made plans to smuggle the precious *Penicillium notatum* mould out of Oxford, hidden in their clothes, if the Nazis should arrive, rather than let the enemy acquire the vital substance. By the autumn of 1940 the Oxford pathology department had been turned into a factory, devoted to making as much

At work during the Second World War

penicillin as possible for human trials. And the team published a paper, entitled, 'Penicillin as a Chemo-therapeutic Agent', in *The Lancet*. One of those who read it was Alexander Fleming.

He had not previously known of the new research, but now he went off to Oxford to call on the team. 'I've come to see what you've been doing with my old penicillin', he told Florey. Whilst the Oxford research was in progress, Fleming had been carrying on with his own wartime work at St Mary's, ignoring the bombs falling on London. But although he played no part in the labours of Florey and Chain, he soon had a chance to use their new penicillin drug on a patient.

In the summer of 1942 a member of the optical firm owned by John and Robert Fleming became dangerously ill with meningitis (a bacterial infection). At Robert's request, he was admitted to St Mary's, under Alec's care. Penicillin still only existed in minute, precious quantities, but Florey gave some to Fleming for his patient — who made a miraculous recovery.

At the time, the war was going badly for Britain and the Allies, and the newspapers were filled with reports of battles and bombing; but on 27 August 1942, *The Times* carried a more hopeful news-story. Headed 'Penicillium', it was a simple account of the new healing substance undergoing trials in Oxford. No people's names were mentioned. At once, Sir Almroth Wright sent off a letter to *The Times*, stating that the credit for the drug should be given to Alexander Fleming, 'For he is the discoverer of penicillin . . .'. From then on, the publicity bandwagon which was to follow Fleming for

51

Penicillin 'factory' at the Sir William Dunn School of Pathology in 1949

the rest of his life began to roll, as the press, eager for some good news, seized on the story of the 'wonderdrug' and its quiet Scots creator. Florey would have nothing to do with the press. He disliked publicity, and had no wish to arouse hopes in sick people for whom there was, as yet, no penicillin generally available. And so it was Alec Fleming who became the great media figure — photographed, interviewed and reported across the world.

In the USA, as in Britain, excitement over the new drug began to mount, with most of the credit going to Fleming. American and Canadian scientists helped in Florey's work, and the American Rockefeller Foundation provided him with vital research funds. But it was Fleming, discoverer of the original mould, whose picture appeared on the cover of America's prestigious *Time* magazine. The respected bacteriologist had become a celebrity.

With the large-scale production of penicillin, towards the end of the war, its powers were proved beyond any doubt. Sickness and infection among the troops were miraculously reduced; the threat of wound infection was lifted. Not only the Allied troops, but the public, too, could now be treated effectively with penicillin — and the door was open to a whole new field of 'antibiotic' drugs.

The world showed its gratitude. In July 1944, Alexander Fleming and Howard Florey were knighted by King George VI. And a year later, as war gave way to peace, Fleming, Florey and Chain flew to Stockholm, in Sweden, to receive one of mankind's highest honours — the Nobel Prize for medicine. Sir Alexander Fleming had come a long way since his barefoot days on a Scottish hill farm.

8 A Happy Ending

'Everywhere I go, people thank me for saving their lives', Fleming once said. 'I don't know why. Nature makes penicillin; I just found it.' In spite of all the honours, rewards, decorations and praise that were heaped upon him, Alec Fleming remained his old modest, humorous self. He always stressed that he had only found penicillin, and Florey had made it a practical reality; and he insisted that chance, or Fate, had brought about the discovery. When the great President de Gaulle of France presented him with the medal of a Commander of the Legion of Honour, Fleming pointed out to his French hosts, 'But for Pasteur, I should be nothing.'

Fleming's papal medal

Nevertheless, he much enjoyed his new role. In England he carried on with his daily routine at St Mary's. One interviewer arrived to see the great man, only to find him white-coated in his little laboratory, brewing up tea over a bunsen-burner, quite unaffected by his fame. But he happily kept scrapbooks of his press-cuttings, particularly the wildly inaccurate ones, and he flew all over the world, delivering lectures, visiting universities, and receiving awards. He met kings, presidents and popes; at a football match in Spain, the whole 20,000-strong crowd rose and applauded when Sir Alexander and Lady Fleming took their seats; in the United States he was made an Honorary Chief of the Kiowa Indian tribe, and in 1951 the students of Edinburgh University elected him their rector. Everywhere, crowds turned out to cheer and applaud the man who had helped to bring new hope of life and health to humanity.

For Alec, one of the most moving occasions came when he made an official visit to his old home town of Darvel. The little town turned out in force to greet him, with pipers playing, newsreel cameras whirring and all the local dignitaries present, to hear him make a speech in which he recalled his early life amongst them all. At Lochfield Farm, on 'the moors beyond', Flemings still lived and farmed — for Alec's brother Hugh had bought the farm — and it remained in the family for many years.

One great sorrow came to mar these years of success: late in 1949, after a severe illness, his wife Sareen died. Alec missed her desperately. He immersed himself in

As Rector of Edinburgh University

his work at St Mary's — and now, colleagues saw, he kept the door of his laboratory shut.

It was through his work that a new, and unexpected, joy came into Alec's life. Among his team at St Mary's there was a Greek woman doctor named Dr Amalia Voureka. She was clever, beautiful, and an exceptional personality, who had played an active part in the Greek war-time resistance against the Nazis. With Fleming, she had been researching into an organism called 'Proteus vulgaris', on which they published a learned paper in 1950.

Gradually, after Sareen died, the professional respect which Fleming felt for Dr Voureka began to turn into friendship. She accompanied him to one or two public functions, and they found they enjoyed each other's company. Invited down to The Dhoon in the summer of 1951, Amalia Voureka entered completely into the spirit of the place — gardening, fishing, joining in all the games, and carrying out experiments of her own in the little laboratory which Alec had built in the garden. When Dr Voureka returned to work in Greece, at the end of the year, Alec seemed lost. But they kept in touch, and their story ended happily: in April 1953 they were married, at Chelsea Register Office.

Fleming was almost seventy-two, his wife some thirty years younger, but the age-gap was unimportant. They were ideally matched, and very happy. With the new Lady Fleming at his side Alec seemed to enjoy life more than ever, and together they undertook endless tours — to Cuba, to Brazil, to the USA, where they had many friends. When the end came for Alexander

Alec and Amalia in the garden at The Dhoon

The mould *Penicillium notatum* as seen under a microscope

Fleming, with a sudden heart attack on 11 March 1955, Amalia was with him, at their home in Chelsea.

Tributes poured in from every corner of the globe. Many cities and villages in Europe today have a 'Rua Fleming', or a Fleming Square, to commemorate his contribution to mankind. In St Mary's Hospital, Paddington a plaque marks the room where he made his discovery; while outside, passers-by in Praed Street can look up at the third-floor turret room of the hospital, and imagine the short, quiet Scotsman at his cluttered bench.

59

A simple memorial outside Lochfield Farm; a marble slab where Fleming lies in St Paul's Cathedral; buildings, statues and street names all honour the memory of the great Scottish bacteriologist who found penicillin. But most important are the millions of people, throughout the world, who owe their health to Alexander Fleming's discovery. They are his greatest memorial.